D1365854

LL Cool J

by Z.B. Hill

Superstars of Hip-Hop

Alicia Keys

Beyoncé

Black Eyed Peas

Ciara

Dr. Dre

Drake

Eminem

50 Cent

Flo Rida

Hip Hop:
A Short History

Jay-Z

Kanye West

Lil Wayne

LL Cool J

Ludacris

Mary J. Blige

Notorious B.I.G.

Rihanna

Sean "Diddy" Combs

Snoop Dogg

T.I.

T-Pain

Timbaland

Tupac

Usher

LL Cool J

by Z.B. Hill

Mason Crest

Chapter 1

"Greatest of All Time"

It's 2005, and LL Cool J is performing at the Hammerstein Ballroom in New York City. He's dressed in classic Cool J fashion: a white Kangol hat, a thick gold chain, and no shirt. Everyone is cheering. People are screaming his name. With a big smile on his face, he begins to let loose rhymes.

A Living Legend

LL Cool J has been in the game for a long time. He released his first album in 1985. Since that day, he's never slowed down. He's made twelve major albums in his career. He's become a successful movie actor. And he's even found time to act in a TV show and give to **charity**.

But on that night in 2005, LL was there not to perform. He was there to be honored. It was the *Second Annual Hip-Hop Honors* show. It celebrated the music of hip-hop superstars. LL Cool J, Big Daddy Kane, Ice-T, and other stars were invited.

The show made it clear just how famous LL had become. Other hip-hop stars, like Nelly, performed LL's music. Over the years, LL has become the star that other artists look up to. He's **inspired** many people. That night, Nelly performed LL's song "I'm Bad." He did a great job. A reporter asked him how he was able to sound so much like LL. "Man, I've been doing LL my whole life," Nelly told the reporter.

LL is more than a good rapper. For many in the hip-hop game, he's also a hero.

LL Cool J (center) signs a new record deal with Def Jam Music in 2003; Def Jam founder Russell Simmons is seated on the left. LL was Def Jam's first big star, and his popularity made the label among the most important in hip-hop.

LL Cool J

Mason Crest
370 Reed Road
Broomall, Pennsylvania 19008
www.masoncrest.com

Printed and bound in the United States of America.

First printing
9 8 7 6 5 4 3 2 1

Library of Congress Cataloging-in-Publication Data

Hill, Z. B.
  LL Cool J / by Z.B. Hill.
     p. cm. – (Superstars of hip-hop)
  Includes index.
  ISBN 978-1-4222-2522-6 (hard cover) – ISBN 978-1-4222-2508-0 (series hardcover) – ISBN 978-1-4222-9224-2 (ebook)
  1. LL Cool J, 1968–-Juvenile literature. 2. Rap musicians–United States–Biography–Juvenile literature. I. Title.
  ML3930.L115H55 2012
  782.421649092–dc23
  [B]
                               2011019647

Produced by Harding House Publishing Services, Inc.
www.hardinghousepages.com
Interior Design by MK Bassett-Harvey.
Cover design by Torque Advertising & Design.

Publisher's notes:
 • All quotations in this book come from original sources and contain the spelling and grammatical inconsistencies of the original text.
 • The Web sites mentioned in this book were active at the time of publication. The publisher is not responsible for Web sites that have changed their addresses or discontinued operation since the date of publication. The publisher will review and update the Web site addresses each time the book is reprinted.

DISCLAIMER: The following story has been thoroughly researched, and to the best of our knowledge, represents a true story. While every possible effort has been made to ensure accuracy, the publisher will not assume liability for damages caused by inaccuracies in the data, and makes no warranty on the accuracy of the information contained herein. This story has not been authorized nor endorsed by LL Cool J.

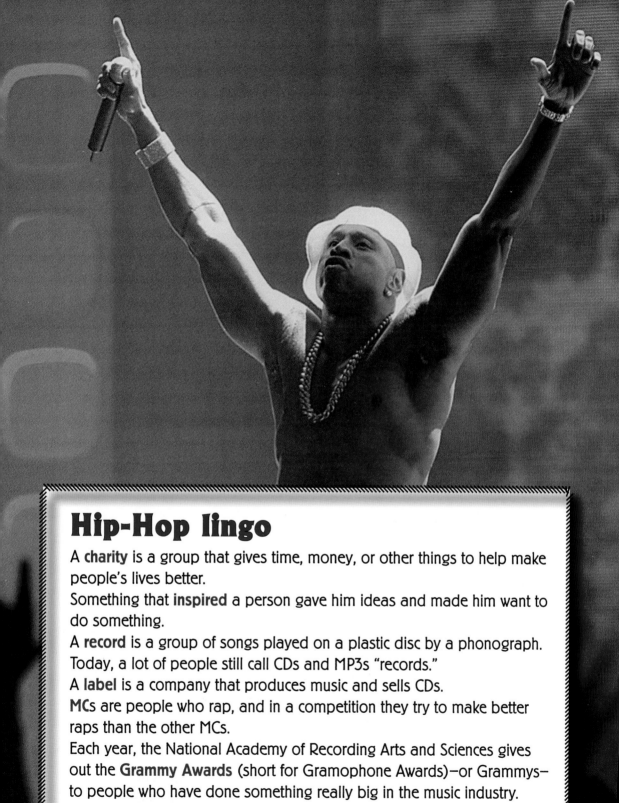

Hip-Hop lingo

A **charity** is a group that gives time, money, or other things to help make people's lives better.

Something that **inspired** a person gave him ideas and made him want to do something.

A **record** is a group of songs played on a plastic disc by a phonograph. Today, a lot of people still call CDs and MP3s "records."

A **label** is a company that produces music and sells CDs.

MCs are people who rap, and in a competition they try to make better raps than the other MCs.

Each year, the National Academy of Recording Arts and Sciences gives out the **Grammy Awards** (short for Gramophone Awards)—or Grammys—to people who have done something really big in the music industry.

Contents

1. "Greatest of All Time"   **7**

2. In the Beginning: Queens   **11**

3. "Just Knock Them Out"   **19**

4. Mr. Smith   **25**

5. A Living Legend   **37**

Time Line   **42**

Discography   **45**

Find Out More   **46**

Index   **47**

About the Author   **48**

Picture Credits   **48**

I Need a Label

When he got his first **record** deal, LL was just 16 years old. He was a skinny kid with a big dream. He signed with a brand-new **label** called Def Jam. More than 23 years later, he was still making albums for Def Jam. And they were still selling millions of copies.

Over the years, the **MC** with a big heart and a big smile has also made big waves in the music business. He's won **Grammy Awards**. He's overcome nearly every challenge in his life.

And yet it wasn't an easy ride. Along the way, LL has had to battle many enemies, including himself. He's struggled with the dangers of money and fame. He's worked hard to be a good husband and father. Through it all, he's become a better man. He's come out on the other side a hip-hop star that everyone can look at and admire.

So how did it all begin?

Hip-Hop lingo

If someone is being **abusive** to someone, it means that person is hurting her and treating her badly.

A **mixer** is a piece of equipment that takes the signals coming from different instruments and microphones and puts them together so they can be recorded.

DJ is short for disc jockey. A DJ plays music on the radio or at a party and announces the songs.

Lyrics are the words in a song.

A **demo** is a rough, early version of a CD before the real thing comes out.

A **producer** is the person in charge of putting together songs. A producer makes the big decisions about the music.

Debut is another word for first.

An album goes **platinum** when it sells more than 1,000,000 copies.

Chapter 2

In the Beginning: Queens

LL Cool J was born James Todd Smith on January 14, 1968, in Brentwood, Long Island. In the early days, he was known by his middle name, Todd. Sadly, he was born into a violent home. Early in his life, his mother separated from his father, James. He was an **abusive** husband. Ondrea didn't want to raise her son like that.

LL Cool J's story is surprising in a lot of ways. No one might guess, for example, that one of LL's heroes is his grandmother, Ellen Griffin. She is an amazing woman who in many ways saved LL's career. Young Todd loved to visit his grandparents in Queens. Their house was a place of love and safety for him. His real home was not such a pleasant place. So when Todd was told he'd be moving into their house for good, he was very happy.

Ellen and her husband, Eugene, took Todd and his mother, Ondrea, into their home. But it seemed that even his grandparents couldn't keep him safe from his father.

Violent Days

One night, while Ondrea and Todd were staying in Queens, James decided to pay a visit. He wanted Ondrea to take him back. She refused, and this made James very angry. He pulled out a gun and started shooting. Todd was asleep when the gunshots woke him up. He ran into the next room and saw blood. His mother and his grandpa had both been shot.

Somehow, Ellen Griffin carried both her husband and daughter to the backseat of her car. She drove them to the hospital. Doctors spent hours patching up their wounds. They both survived. Eugene came home from the hospital after a few weeks. Ondrea took longer to heal. But she got better too, and left the hospital after six months.

In the meantime, James had run to California to escape arrest. But Ondrea told the police she didn't want her ex-husband behind bars. Somehow, she was able to forgive him. James was never put in jail for his actions.

Todd and Ondrea's problems didn't end there. Ondrea married another abusive man named Roscoe. He was nice to Ondrea but very mean to Todd. When LL grew up, he wrote a book about his life. In it, he tells how Roscoe hit him with his fists. Sometimes, he used extension cords and parts of vacuum cleaners to beat Todd. One time, Roscoe threw Todd outside without a coat on a cold winter day. Todd hadn't done anything wrong. He'd just asked for something to eat.

Those were not good years. But out of young Todd's pain would come a beautiful thing—music.

Two Turntables and a Microphone

For Todd, music was like a breath of fresh air. The first time he heard rap music, he was hooked. He knew there was something special about it. His grandparents saw his interest in music and wanted to help. So they bought him a set of speakers, a **mixer**, and a microphone. It was everything he needed to start making music.

In those days, every rapper needed a **DJ**. A DJ created beats for MCs to rhyme over. Todd found the best DJ in Queens, a young man named Jay Philpot. The two quickly became friends. Soon, they were performing together at neighborhood parties.

They also made tapes of their music. At this point, Todd gave himself the name Ladies Love Cool James. He and Jay sent their tapes to many labels. They hoped that someone would like their music. But no one was interested in putting money into an un-known rapper. Then, one day, a young producer named Rick Ru-

Russell Simmons and Rick Rubin founded the Def Jam music label in the early 1980s, signing LL Cool J as their first act. Simmons and Rubin are in the center of this 2001 photo with rappers Noreaga (now called NORE) and Capone.

bin heard one of LL's tapes. He liked it a lot. He wanted to meet the man behind the music.

When LL met Rubin, he was surprised to find a white Jewish man. ("Yo! I thought you were black!" was the first thing he said.) But LL and his new partner quickly got to work. Rubin played some of his own beats for LL. He liked what he heard and started writing **lyrics** to go with the beats. Rubin told LL what he liked and didn't like. LL made some changes. In no time, they had a **demo** they both were excited about.

But what about LL's name? Rubin thought "Ladies Love Cool James" was too long. He asked if LL could make it shorter. "I was like, whatever," LL told CNN years later. "It could have been whatever he wanted it to be, you know. I'd have still made the album." LL just wanted to make music. He took Rubin's advice and shortened his name to LL Cool J.

They also needed a **producer**. Rubin tracked down a friend of his named Russell Simmons. Rubin and Simmons wanted to start their own label. With LL on their team, they finally decided to launch Def Jam records. LL's song "I Need a Beat" was their first hit song.

It was also the first single off his **debut** album, *Radio*. Along with a few other tracks, "I Need a Beat" put LL and Def Jam on the map. In just a few months, they were famous. LL was still a young man, only 16 years old. He couldn't believe what was happening. In his book, he talks about hearing himself on the radio for the first time. "It was like time had slowed down. The earth was spinning half time and it was just me and my record."

No one was more thrilled about this good news than Ellen Griffin. She was happy for her grandson but also worried. LL was going to fewer and fewer classes at school. It was hard for him to care about his grades. Ellen did not want him to give up on high school.

So she put her foot down. She told him he had to move out of the house if he was going to skip classes. LL chose music over school and moved out.

Later in life, he regretted this decision. But at the time, it seemed to make sense. The cash was starting to come in. LL was living his dream.

Trouble at the Top

In 1987, it was time for another hit album. LL dropped *Bigger and Deffer* on his fans. It was a big hit. So big, in fact, that it went double **platinum**!

LL Cool J poses with Bobcat, E. Love, and Cut Creator backstage at the 1988 Soul Train Music Awards program. That night LL Cool J won for the crossover single "I Need Love" and the double platinum album *Bigger and Deffer.*

LL took a different approach on *Bigger*. He decided to try a few love songs. Rubin and Simmons had their doubts. They didn't like their star rapper showing his softer side. But the songs worked. LL's softer side brought him even more fans.

Love was on LL's mind a lot during those days. In 1987, he met Simone Johnson, his first steady girlfriend. The two had much in common. They grew up in the same neighborhood. They knew a lot of the same pain. Even so, LL had a hard time being good to Simone. His rap career kept him away from home for long stretches of time. He wasn't always faithful to her.

LL had money troubles, too. With fame came big paychecks. LL was not ready for the big responsibilities. LL talks about those days in his book. He wrote that he would walk into car dealerships and buy a new Porsche or BMW—right on the spot!

From the moment they met in 1987, LL Cool J and Simone Johnson were meant to be together. They were not married until 1995, however. By that time, Simone and LL had two children and a third on the way.

The release of *Bigger and Deffer* made LL Cool J a rich man. He was making more money than either he or his staff knew how to handle. The addition of his estranged father to the management team did not help the situation.

LL had no one to give him good advice. He had made his mother the manager of his money. When things got too confusing, she decided to call her ex-husband. He wasn't LL's favorite person, but he did know a lot about money. Hoping his dad could help him, LL agreed. As it later turned out, this was another bad choice.

Things kept getting worse. He made his third album, called *Walking With a Panther*. But it didn't sell as well as his first two albums. He also started using drugs. LL says that this was one of the worst times of his life. He was throwing away his chance to live a good life.

In 1989, his girlfriend gave birth to a son, named Najee. LL faced many questions. Would he be a good father? Would he turn his music career in a better direction?

Hip-Hop lingo

The **Qur'an** is the holy book for the religion of Islam.
When someone is **abandoned**, he is left on his own, without help.

Chapter 3

"Just Knock Them Out"

At the end of the 1980s, a new kind of hip-hop appeared. It was called gangsta rap. It sold millions of records and changed hip-hop in big ways. Gangstas rapped about violence and life on the streets. Many people began to doubt rappers like LL Cool J. They saw him as weak, as not having a hard edge to his music.

LL knew he would have to prove them wrong, but how? Surprisingly, the answer came from his grandma, Ellen. She thought worrying about other people's opinions was silly. She told LL, "Oh, baby, just knock them out!" Little did she know, that's exactly what her grandson was going to do.

He called his next album *Mama Said Knock You Out*. It was LL's answer to gangsta rap. In his words, it was "not gangsta, just hard." The album won LL a Grammy for Best Rap Solo Performance. This was a huge honor. LL was on top of the world. But he didn't stop there.

He decided to start acting in movies. A lot of hip-hop stars try to be actors. Very rarely do they turn out to be any good, though. But LL proved to be a talented actor. In 1991, he starred in the movie *The*

Hard Way. The next year, he landed another big part in the movie *Toys*. It seemed there was nothing LL couldn't do!

Living a Better Life

Seen from the outside, LL had the perfect life. He'd saved his music career and launched his acting career. He had a steady flow of money coming in. But inside, LL was struggling with some of life's biggest questions.

By 1990, LL had a son and a daughter with his girlfriend, Simone. Because of his busy life, he rarely spent time with them. He

Thanks to his mentor Charles Fisher, LL Cool J began exploring his spirituality. Fisher helped the rapper recognize his personal problems. His darkest album, *14 Shots to the Dome*, became part of his soul-searching effort.

By 1990 LL Cool J's career seemed in need of a boost—*Rolling Stone* noted that there were "insults to be avenged." The rapper's album *Mama Said Knock You Out*, inspired by advice from his grandmother, proved that LL was still a rapper with attitude.

was becoming the kind of father he didn't want to be. To make things worse, he was also seeing other women. He wasn't being faithful to Simone.

But into this mess stepped a helpful man named Charles Fisher. He urged LL to see the mistakes in his life, and LL listened. In

LL Cool J has had one of the longest-lived careers in the hop-hop world. However, the rapper's detractors have always been ready to claim that LL was washed up—a charge he attempted to answer with his album *Mr. Smith* (1995).

his book, LL writes about that period of his life. For a time, he said, he had thought he was living well. "But underneath the gold chains and the glitter was this foul stench," he wrote. "And I guess Charles smelled it." LL even compared himself to a drug addict, or "junkie." He said he was like "a junkie needing a fix, and [Charles] had the drug—knowledge."

Charles asked LL to try reading some religious books. At first, LL wasn't too excited about the idea. But then he began reading the Bible, the **Qur'an**, and other books Charles suggested. He also took Charles' advice to help out in his community. LL became a leader for Youth Enterprises, a program for poor kids. It was a life-changing experience for him. From then on, he decided to commit a lot of his money and time to helping kids.

14 Shots

A lot of good things came out of that difficult time in LL's life. In his book, he remembers breaking down in tears. "I was crying for a woman I had treated like a dog, crying for the children I had **abandoned**, crying for my life, which I was just throwing away." But those old ways were coming to an end.

LL called his next album *14 Shots to the Dome*. It had some of his darkest and deepest lyrics yet. LL searched within himself and put some of his own stories into his songs.

Sadly, listeners weren't ready for the new LL. They wanted more of his old party jams. *14 Shots* didn't sell as well as past albums.

But that didn't bother LL. He had other things on his mind. For one, he realized he couldn't always count on platinum record sales. More than ever, he needed good advice for how to use his money. He knew he couldn't depend on his father. He would have to do it himself. At the age of 27, LL was ready to go back to school. It was the beginning of a lot of changes in LL's life.

Hip-Hop lingo

A **studio** is a place where musicians go to record their music and turn it into CDs.

When someone's love is **unconditional**, it means that a person doesn't need to earn it or behave in a certain way to receive it.

Profanity is using curse words and other words that might offend people.

Chapter 4

Mr. Smith

1995 was an important year for LL. He was ready to be Todd Smith again. He'd put off a lot of big decisions for a long time. But now he was ready. He fired his father. He went back to school to get his high school diploma. And then he made an even bigger decision. He married his girlfriend, the mother of his two children.

LL was happy to marry Simone. "I realized that the love I was seeking was there all along," he said. "It had been there for more than eight years." They were married in August of 1995. It was a small, simple wedding. Soon after, Simone had their third child, a daughter named Samaria. Before LL knew it, he was a full-time dad.

His decision to go back to school made his grandma very happy. It was a tough decision for someone with as much fame and money as LL. But he did it anyway. He wanted to learn how to be smarter about his money. To do that, he needed an education.

Another Good Break

One good decision followed another. LL's next move was to put his acting career on a better track. In 1995, he got a starring role in a

At the premiere of *Deliver Us from Eva*, LL Cool J poses with fellow rapper Will Smith. Smith had gone from a career in rap music to starring roles in television shows and movies and LL hoped to emulate him.

TV show! It was called *In the House.* LL played an ex-football star named Marion Hill. He loved playing Marion because he was a positive, friendly character. In his book, LL wrote that he liked Marion's choices—"no drinking, no wild women, no drugs." The show lasted more than three years. The final episode aired in 1999.

LL kept learning from others. He admired his friend Will Smith a lot. Will had turned his own rap career into an acting career. LL wrote, "Today I see Will Smith in [major] films, having become a box office superstar. And I respect how he [turned] his rap career into a big-time film career."

In the meantime, LL kept pushing his rap skills. He made an album called *Mr. Smith* in 1995. It was yet another hit, selling millions of copies. It also earned LL another Grammy for Best Rap Solo Performance for "Hey Lover." The song proved that LL was still growing. Even after ten years in the game, he still had room to improve.

A Changed Man

LL's life began to settle down. He had a lot of new ideas he wanted to put into action. For starters, he wanted to spend a lot more time helping other people. He began visiting hospitals, schools, and churches in many cities. During one hospital visit, he met a boy who had been badly burned in a fire. "I realized not only that this boy was someone I wanted to look out for, but that there are millions of kids out there, and they're all special," he wrote.

It was a new page in the story of LL's life. He was a happy father, a TV star, and he was working to make others' lives better. When he won that second Grammy, everything seemed to fall into place. LL described himself as a boxer who gets back his title. "The feeling of winning that Grammy—it was like regaining the heavyweight championship of the world."

Writing His Story

With so many years of work behind him, it made sense for LL to take a break and look back at his life. He decided to do that by writing a book. He called it *I Make My Own Rules*.

LL wrote the book to tell his life's story. But he also wrote it for kids. He wanted them to see the mistakes he'd made in his life. He wanted them to lead better lives. LL spoke out to kids who have felt the pain of abuse. He wanted them to know that they are not alone. By telling his own story, he hoped to inspire others.

LL also focused on the dangers of drugs. He admitted to using drugs and even selling them for a while. But he warned others not to follow in his footsteps. "The dealer's life has many entrances. But the only two exits are prison and death. Remember that," he wrote.

LL's book came at a time when hip-hop was hurting from the deaths of two of its biggest stars. Only a year before his book came out, Tupac and Biggie had both been killed. LL wanted to set the record straight. He pointed out that hip-hop wasn't the real problem. He pointed to crime, poverty, joblessness and the other dangers of America's city streets. He said it was wrong to put the blame on hip-hop for the violence in our world.

Back to the Big Screen

With his book done, LL was looking to return to acting. His only starring role up until then had been in *Out-of-Sync*. LL wanted another chance. In 1998, he took parts in *Caught Up* and in a horror movie called *Halloween H2O*. The next year, he got a part in another horror movie, called *Deep Blue Sea*.

But his biggest break was the football movie *Any Given Sunday*. LL had played football as a kid. He really wanted the part. After

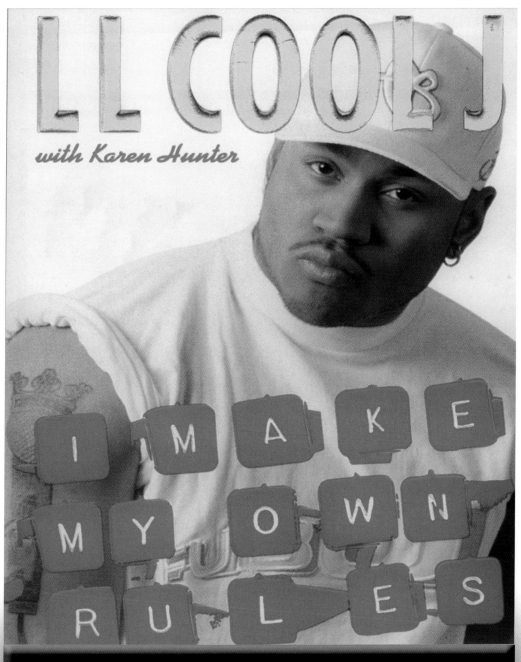

The autobiography *I Make My Own Rules* was LL Cool J's chance to tell his story and explore his life. In the book he described many experiences that he had never previously discussed publicly, such as being beaten as a child.

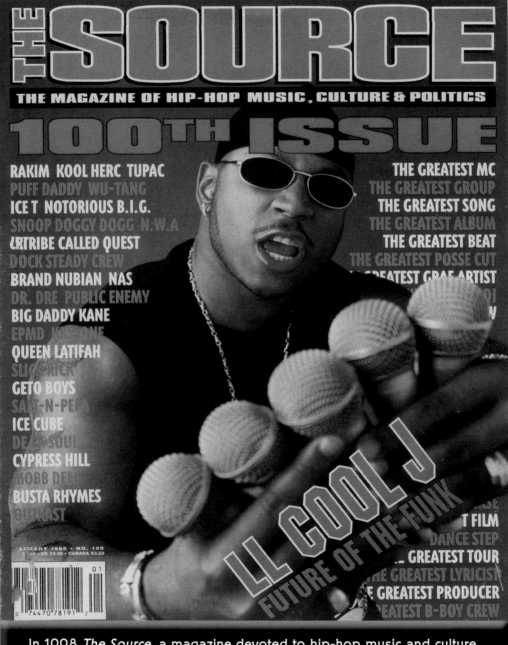

In 1998 *The Source*, a magazine devoted to hip-hop music and culture, featured LL Cool J on the cover of its 100th issue. Ironically, it was this same year that LL decided to refocus his career toward making movies in Hollywood.

LL Cool J had an important part as a football player in the hit movie *Any Given Sunday* (1999). The film was directed by Oliver Stone and also featured award-winning actor Al Pacino and talented comedian Jamie Foxx.

he got it, he did a strict training program to make his body fit and strong. The movie was LL's biggest yet.

Time to Be the Greatest

With a few movies out of the way, LL went back to the **studio**. By 2000, he knew how to run his career. He was finding a balance between music, acting, and family. In 2000, he made an album called *G.O.A.T. Featuring James T. Smith: The Greatest of All Time.*

It was a bold name for a record. But it didn't sell as well as he'd hoped. Even so, it included some of LL's best songs yet. One song

LL Cool J promotes his album *G.O.A.T. Featuring James T. Smith: The Greatest of All Time* at a Boston radio station. The album's title was borrowed from the boxing legend Muhammad Ali, who also called himself the Greatest of All Time.

was especially important. It was called "Big Mama (**Unconditional** Love)." Written for his grandma, Ellen, it told of all the advice she had given him over the years. LL let everyone know just how much this woman had done for him.

And he did it just in time, too. Ellen passed away the next year, in 2002.

A Hip-Hop Role Model

LL wanted to bring even more positive energy to his next album. He told *Billboard* his hopes. He wanted to make "a positive record

The violent and dysfunctional relationship LL Cool J described in "Father" revealed to his fans the terror he had felt as a child. LL was determined not to have that kind of relationship with his own son, Najee.

LL Cool J has long been committed to helping young people. Here, he joins other hip-hop artists at a 2002 rally in New York City to protest cuts in the budgets of city public schools.

with no **profanity**, strong energy, and tight beats; a record that makes [people] feel better after hearing it."

LL was in tune with a lot of people's feelings at the time. Many people wanted to turn hip-hop in a new direction. They wanted hip-hop to speak peace and hope, not hate and violence. In 2001, LL went to a meeting in New York City to discuss how rappers could help young people. It was the first Hip-Hop Summit.

The rappers agreed to send better messages to young people. "It doesn't matter how good you're supposed to be at what you do," LL told *MTV News*. "If you can't inspire people to be positive and be leaders and dream, you're not [using] the power that you have for the best."

Even after so much fame, LL kept a cool head. He saw his place in the bigger picture. He was thankful he still had the chance to make music. He wanted to use that chance to help others. "I'm very appreciative that people can enjoy what I'm doing," he told *Ebony*. "All I can do is just give them the best that I can give them."

Hip-Hop lingo

If a person is considered a **legend**, he is well-known for who he is or what he has done, and his fame is likely to last for a long time.

If something has **longevity**, it will last for a very long time.

Chapter 5

A Living Legend

The last few years have seen LL go from hip-hop star to hip-hop **legend**. He's proven he is here to stay. In the early 2000s, he re-signed with Def Jam. After 20 years, Def Jam and LL teamed up once again. In his time with Def Jam, LL had sold over 20 million records. The owner of Def Jam, Russell Simmons, took time to thank LL for his hard work. He said, "LL Cool J is a shining example of the **longevity** and power of hip-hop."

Another Gift to Kids

In the next few years, LL continued to try new things. In 2002, he made a kid's book. It was called *And the Winner Is.* It was a story about basketball. It invited readers to rap along to the CD that came with the book.

The book combined many of LL's interests. It had great music, a good story, and it helped kids learn. It also inspired kids to make their own raps. LL put some tracks on the CD that were just music with no words. Kids could write their own lyrics and rap over the open beat.

LL Cool J is pictured in a New York bookstore promoting the children's book he wrote to help teach good sportsmanship. The Rawsistaz Reviewers said, "This is an excellent book that [we] would highly recommend for children."

The book proved that hip-hop was gaining fans every day. "Whether you're a fan of the music or not, your kids probably are," he told CNN.

Always the Actor

LL continues to get bigger and better acting roles. In 2003, he did a movie called *Deliver Us from Eva*. He had a starring role. People liked his acting. *Premiere* magazine said that "overall, he delivers a [very] pleasing, touching performance." This was high praise for a rapper-turned-actor.

In 2003 LL Cool J starred as an officer in an elite police S.W.A.T. team opposite Samuel L. Jackson and Colin Ferrell. It was the second film the rapper starred in that year, although neither movie received particularly good reviews.

LL appeared in four more movies over the next four years. One of the biggest was 2003's *S.W.A.T.* Another film, called *Last Holiday*, was also a hit. LL starred beside Queen Latifah. Once again, critics liked his performance.

During these years, LL created his own film company, called LL Cool J Inc. The company would allow LL to support other moviemakers and actors.

In recent years, LL has done a lot of acting on popular TV shows. He's been on *30 Rock*, *House*, and even *Sesame Street*! In 2009, LL began playing Sam Hanna on the show *NCIS: Los Angeles*. Today, many of LL's fans know him more for his acting than his music!

Clothing Line

As usual, LL wasn't happy to just do one thing at a time. So he also created his own clothing line. By then, he was no stranger to fashion. He'd already worked for many years with the streetwear company FUBU. In 2006, he debuted his own line, called Todd Smith.

LL wanted his clothes to be one of a kind. Many hip-hop artists have made everyday street clothes or clothes for the very rich. LL wanted to shoot for the in-between people. He created formal clothes like overcoats and dinner jackets. But he didn't make them too expensive. He wanted people to look rich. He didn't want them to have to be rich to buy his clothes.

For the Love of the Music

LL put out three albums one right after the other. In 2004, he made *The DEFinition*, and in 2006, *Todd Smith*. In 2008, it was *Exit 13*.

Why keep making music? LL has a simple answer—it's what he loves to do! "It soothes and heals my soul," he told *Jet* magazine.

As he gets older, LL asks more artists to join him on his records. He's worked with Mary J. Blige, Ginuwine, and Jennifer Lopez. He's worked with producers Timbaland, Trackmasters, and Pharrel Williams, too.

LL showed his love for the music world when he hosted the 2012 Grammy Awards. The awards show was held on the night after Whitney Houston died. LL made sure to take some time to honor the famous singer. Singer Jennifer Hudson sang one of Whitney's most famous songs, "I Will Always Love You." LL hosted music's biggest award show on a tough night, but he did a great job.

Rapping Into the Future

Today, LL's place at the top of hip-hop is secure. Even artists who LL looked up to as a boy have sung his praises. Grandmaster Flash said this of LL's style: "Love songs? Ain't too many cats who could touch 'em with that." Rick Rubin has called LL's rhymes groundbreaking. "He's the first MC to really take the lyric writing to another level." But Darryl McDaniels, also known as DMC from Run-D.M.C., said it best: "No one can take his crown."

Album after album, year after year, LL Cool J proves himself a hip-hop legend. He's made his share of mistakes. He's seen many hard times. But what makes him different is his attitude. He's turned his failures into successes. And he's found a way to live his life for others, too.

LL Cool J, James Todd Smith, whatever you want to call him—it looks like he's here to stay.

Time Line

1968	James Todd Smith is born on January 14 in Long Island, New York.
1979	He attends his first Sugarhill Gang concert at the Harlem Armory.
1982	Ladies Love Cool J starts performing at block parties with friend Jay Philpot.
1984	He sends a demo to hip-hop producer Rick Rubin, who teams up with Russell Simmons to release "I Need a Beat," Def Jam's first record.
1985	LL releases his first album, *Radio*, and makes a cameo appearance in the film *Krush Groove*.
1986	*Radio* goes gold, and LL appears in the movie *Wildcats*.
1987	He meets Simone, his future wife, and releases *Bigger and Deffer*.
1988	LL records "Going Back to Cali" for the *Less Than Zero* soundtrack.
1989	LL Cool J releases *Walking With a Panther*. Simone gives birth to a son named Najee.
1990	LL finds a mainstream success with his fourth album, *Mama Said Knock You Out*, which features chart-topping songs "Mama Said Knock You Out" and "Around the Way Girl." His daughter, Italia, is born.
1991	He performs on the MTV show *Unplugged* and lands small roles in the movie *The Hard Way*.
1992	The rapper wins his first Grammy for Best Rap Solo performance and opens up Camp Cool J for disadvantaged inner-city kids.

1993 LL takes part in the formation of AmeriCorps, a national volunteer organization. He also releases *14 Shots to the Dome*.

1995 The album *Mr. Smith* is released. LL stars in a new TV sitcom *In The House*. He marries Simone, and his daughter Samaria is born.

1997 LL receives his second Grammy and releases his greatest hits album, *All World*. The album *Phenomenon* is released, and LL publishes his autobiography, *I Make My Own Rules*.

1998 He appears in the urban thriller *Caught Up*, the romantic comedy *Woo*, and the horror flick *Halloween H20*.

1999 The last episode of *In The House* airs. LL lands roles in three more movies, including the blockbuster *Any Given Sunday*.

2000 *G.O.A.T. Featuring James T. Smith: The Greatest of All Time* is released. LL's daughter Nina is born.

2001 LL Cool J attends the first Hip-Hop Summit in New York City.

2002 The album *10* is released, and LL's children's book, *And the Winner Is*, is published.

2003 LL costars in *Deliver Us From Eva* and *S.W.A.T.* He also re-signs with Def Jam.

2004 The *DEFinition* is released.

2005 LL performs and is paid tribute at the VH1 *2ND Annual Hip-Hop Honors*.

2006 He costars in *Last Holiday* starring Queen Latifah and unveils Todd Smith clothing line. He also releases *Todd Smith.*

2008   Cool J attends the sixth annual "Wrap to Rap" benefit for foster children at the Empire Hotel Rooftop.

2009   LL Cool J hosts the "Grammy Nominations Concert Live!"

2010   LL Cool J appears on the People's Choice Awards alongside Queen Latifah.

2012   LL Cool J hosts the Grammy Awards.

Discography

Albums

1985	Radio
1987	Bigger and Deffer
1989	Walking with a Panther
1990	Mama Said Knock You Out
1993	14 Shots to the Dome
1995	Mr. Smith
1996	All World: Greatest Hits
1997	Phenomenon
2000	G.O.A.T. Featuring James T. Smith: The Greatest of All Time
2002	10
2004	The DEFinition
2006	Todd Smith
2008	Exit 13

In Books

Baker, Soren. *The History of Rap and Hip Hop*. San Diego, Calif.: Lucent, 2006.

Comissiong, Solomon W. F. *How Jamal Discovered Hip-Hop Culture*. New York: Xlibris, 2008.

Cornish, Melanie. *The History of Hip Hop*. New York: Crabtree, 2009.

Czekaj, Jef. *Hip and Hop, Don't Stop!* New York: Hyperion, 2010.

Haskins, Jim. *One Nation Under a Groove: Rap Music and Its Roots*. New York: Jump at the Sun, 2000.

Hatch, Thomas. *A History of Hip-Hop: The Roots of Rap*. Portsmouth, N.H.: Red Bricklearning, 2005.

Websites

LL Cool J on AOL Music
music.aol.com/artist/ll-cool-j

LL Cool J on Internet Movie Database
www.imdb.com/name/nm0005112

LL Cool J on MTV
www.mtv.com/music/artist/ll_cool_j/artist.jtml

LL Cool J on StarPulse
www.starpulse.com/Music/LL_Cool_J

Official Site
www.islanddefjam.com/artist/default.aspx?artistID=7309

Index

14 Shots to the Dome 21, 23

Bible 23
Bigger and Deffer 15, 17

charity 6, 7

DJ 10, 13

Fisher, Charles 21
FUBU 40

G.O.A.T. Featuring James T. Smith: The Greatest of All Time 31
Grammys 6, 9, 19, 27

Hammerstein Ballroom 7

Johnson, Simone 16, 20, 21, 25

label 6, 8, 9, 13, 14

Mama Said Knock You Out 19, 20
MC 6, 9, 13, 41

Najee 17
New York City 7, 34, 35

platinum 10, 15, 23
producer 10, 13, 14, 40

Qur'an 18, 23

Radio 14
Rubin, Rick 13, 14, 16, 41
Run-D.M.C. 41

Smith, Will 26, 27
studio 24, 31

Walking With a Panther 17

About the Author

Z.B. Hill is a an author and publicist living in Binghamton, New York. He has a special interest in adolescent education and how music can be used in the classroom.

Picture Credits

Alecsey Boldeskul/NY Photo Press: p. 38
AP Photo/Bob Galbraith: p. 15
Columbia Pictures/Zuma Press: p. 52
Dreamstime, Sbukely: p. 1
KRT/Olivier Douliery: p. 16
Mario Anzuoni/Splash News: p. 33
Mel Nudelman/PRNewsFoto/NMI: p. 8
NMI/Michelle Feng: p. 29, 30
Reuters/Seth Wenig: p. 6
Sam Mircovich/Reuters: p. 18
Tom Lau/Loud & Clear/Star Max: p. 24
UPI/Ezio Petersen: p. 34, 36
UPI/Michael Germana: p. 33, 52
Warner Bros./Zuma Press: p. 43
Zuma Press/Def Jam: p. 10, 20, 21, 22,
Zuma Press/Rahav Segev: p. 13
Zuma Press/Steven Tackeff: p. 32
Zuma Press/Toronto Star: p. 17

To the best knowledge of the publisher, all other images are in the public domain. If any image has been inadvertently uncredited, please notify Harding House Publishing Services, Vestal, New York 13850, so that rectification can be made for future printings.